Watching

Waves

Watching Waves

Collected Poems
Volume 3

Richard Gartee

LAKE & EMERALD PUBLICATIONS

Published by Lake and Emerald Publications, LLC
www.lepublications.com

Library of Congress Control Number: 2013918810

Paperback ISBN: 978-0-9895104-5-5

Cover Photo: Richard Gartee

Selected poems in this anthology were previously published in *Ann Arbor Review, Chris-Alice, Black Cover Anthology*, and *Chrysalis*. Copyright 1968, 1974, 1975, 1976, 1978, 1979, 1990, 2009

for God
and Guru

Contents

Preface

When it comes down to it, what is more important than knowing who we really are? I don't mean our personality or personal history or genealogy. I mean who is listening to our thoughts, who is aware of our feelings? The experiential evidence says that I am in here, looking out there. At least that was true for me.

I think poets notice their interior processes – if not in real-time, at least when they go back and read what they have written. And for me, there were interior experiences to be explored beyond poetic themes of falling in love or breaking up.

I took an interest in the sutras of Lao Tzu and the Zen of *Cold Mountain Poems*. I began to study meditation and eastern philosophy. I was fortunate to live in a new age dispensation that brought distant Gurus, Tibetan Lamas, Sufi, and Christian mystics into my life. They broadened my viewpoint and led me to seek something deeper.

I found who was in here looking out, and began to write more poems about that. You will find them peppered throughout all my poetry collections. However, this collection is different in that it is comprised almost entirely of deeply personal interior musings about the nature of reality. Themes of a universal God and our search for God are prevalent throughout this collection. Frequently these are expressed in three- or four- line sutras. The opening stanza of the title poem conveys the essential ontology of the book, "We are the observer, seated in Self, watching the universe as a wave flowing before our consciousness."

Over eighty percent of this collection has never appeared in print before. A few poems appeared in *Black Cover Anthology*. The Christmas poems at the end of the book were previously published in chap books, *Ann Arbor Review*, or as individual poems at various Christmases. Although some of the Christmas poems are more nostalgic than the majority of this book, the spiritual nature of Christmas made it seem right to include them.

I do have a couple of notes before you start reading. First is about the use of the pronoun "you." I realize its use made some of the poems seem didactic, but that was not my intent. In most of places the "you" is me; a reflection of my higher-self writing to my lower-self. Please read it from that perspective. I also want to mention that the Roman numerals in several poem titles were not in the original titles. These were added when assembling the collected poem volumes to resolve cases where different poems had duplicate titles.

Finally, I want to acknowledge Marilyn Barnett, a friend who lived at the Temple of the Universe before it was called that. She began helping me edit and organize this collection many years ago. Although she is not around anymore, I hope she will be pleased to see how it turned out.

—Richard Gartee, 2013

Intro Poem

(This poem was originally intended as an introduction to the book long before there was a preface. I chose to keep it anyway.)

Jesus, how could I have forgotten
I walked out the room
and started to laugh

I open my mind
and outlay the book
without any hesitation

I find myself in the midst
of exactly the best resource
for this book
at this precise moment,
to set it down

I owe a lot to Lao Tzu
and to the wise men
I have experienced in this life
but it is Lao Tzu who said what is real
has no name
and what is named ceases to be real
(I'm paraphrasing here)

Endeavor as I have
to set down what I've been shown,
I'm afraid I must admit
that whatever real, that was turned to words
has lost the vibrant life it had on its own

So, this has value only if it serves you.

Watching Waves

We are the observer
seated in Self
watching the universe
as a wave flowing
before our consciousness

There is no past.
It is dead.
Just an image
of where a wave
has gone before.

Einstein imagined
moving at the speed of light.

Riding a beam of light,
what would you see?

Now imagine creation
is a constantly expressing wave
of energy.
And imagine that energy and consciousness
are the same.
What is the experience
of observing the universe as the wave of creation?

Creation is an instantaneous process.
Every second is a new creation.
Every second, the previous state has ceased.

Master

I hear the master of my ship
when the winds howl upon
the stormy sea
and the waves beat the wooden sides
and the rudder jerks from my grip
and turns the prow
from south to north to east

I hear your stars speaking direction
in my inner mind
and the sails bend to your pole
as I leave the world behind
hoping for a land of light
where you set me upon the shore

As I look around with new found
wonder
I marvel at the sight
to discover, that the journeys' end
is but the very land we departed
and it is I, not the world, which turned
around this journey home.

Write More Than You Read

"Write more than you read,"
he said,
"spend twice as much time"

Or that's the way I remember him.
But poems are getting
in mighty short supply around here

I've noticed,
but I'm trying to correct that
with love.

Holiness

There is nothing our
holiness cannot do
its aura extending
infinite distances
in every direction
enveloping
blessing
all who are touched
by it.

Time

In time
we exist
for and with each other
but in timelessness
we exist
as God.

You Are Worthy of Love

I honor you because you are loveable.
Dispel illusions about yourself
and perceive the light within you
the children of God are holy
In this order
you are perfect
worthy of love and honor.

Of Love and Flowers

Of a love affair between
the earth and sun
happens in the flowering
of spring,
when you, as they, were born

The eyes of life
in blossoms open, and
they light the day

Warming the earth,
the sun moves the wind
which carries the fragrance

Their scent is love's color
and its song
their movements
are love's dance
and you
its flower
are the heart
from where love comes

So love
like a flower
loves the sun,
turn toward love
and be warm

love as though
we all
are one
and be of love
as a flower is
a child of the sun.

My Temple

I have known two temples,
one visible
one invisible;
one the body senses,
one the Spirit visualizes.

In the one,
the reasoning identifies and
integrates
the other,
the soul recognizes and absorbs
On the day I realize my power
to overlap these two,
I know I am
the temple.

Perfection

I saw in my Guru great perfection
in subtle realms he moved
with equanimity and intricate timing
the very force of love

and in him I saw him
make me
into his own reflection
and my very essence
being love.

Mahasamadhi

Oh Lord
on this day you have ascended
to meet your Master
let us ascend to the spiritual eye
this day to meet you.

Concentration

Concentration
is everything
Humanity

Put everything
in a single bag
and watch it
do its thing
Humanity

The door stands
always open
the light
through its frame falls
in patterns on the floor
for Humanity.

God

I searched for you everywhere
until I found you.

Once I found you,
I found you everywhere.

Meditation

Beside you
the world quickly pales,
loses its glitter,
and fails to occupy my mind.

Inside of God
I experience unity;
separation ceases
and I feel our one being.

Inside of God
there is only one thing.
Inside of God
we are really one being.
Inside of God
there is no separation.
Inside,
there is nothing outside
of you.

Choices

All my life there are decisions
I see the choices breakdown
into two:

for God
and not for God

that is all
the choice is that simple
every time, every case
if it's not working,
change your choice.

Going Alone

I am going alone
into god.
I have awaited my
companions,
and yet we are each
alone.

And it is God alone
from whom,
we are being
God
and God alone.

Inward

When all else is gone
why look to anything
but meditation
anything but the path
to God?

Inward
if this is going to work
at all
it is certainly, in times of difficulty,
that must
inward
be the first direction turned.

Awareness

What God wants is our attention
focused awareness of what is
at the moment going on
not doing anything to it
just witnessing it transpire
just witnessing from whence it arises
letting it pass when it has passed on

Seeing this moment
the world has nothing to do with you
yet the seeing or not seeing
is all about you

Eventually letting the seeing
show you the roots of the weeds
that spring in the field
of observation
are within you
obstructing the object of consciousness
and diffusing the focus

Only two things are required
that we pay attention
to everything that occurs
in the moment it does so
and when the source of consciousness
becomes the focus of awareness
we surrender to its attraction
to be drawn near.

I Am the Needle

I am the needle
on the pine
the lines of shadows
on the road
and the sun of the morning.

Breathing in your fragrance
I remember you.
With every breath
I hear the sound of your name.

Love II

Love is the sound
of our breath
moving
in and out of
God's body.

Birthday

As the newness comes
I am reborn.
I see the experience of my birth
in the heart of The Lord.

I fold my holiness around
an embryo light
and breathe into it
movement of life-force
up spiral stairs
from the dark
into the sun.

Ecstasy

I am sustained by the love of God
my body is made of
particles of His light
which dance toward you
in a fiery rainbow of brilliance,
His blessing and grace
pulsing in a shimmering dance.

Ecstasy, experiencing
the quiet observation
of these feelings flowing,
just flowing.

I Forgive You

I forgive you
when you are not there
and I only have you inside my head to talk to
and I am thereby forgiven

I pry apart the closed gates of my heart
and open my heart
to remember myself
as love
for love itself has
created me like itself
and only ego
has closed the doors.

Light

Light,
shining into darkness,
forgives the night
its shadowy moments

Light
its whole function
disperses darkness
and dismisses the subject
as unreal

My light
is the reality as sure
as love opens the heart
and illuminates the eyes

With a brush of forgiveness
the world is complete,
illusion is dismissed
and the heart is our home

Remembering the self as light;
Light being our whole function,
the only purpose for being here,
Darkness is dispelled.
by the very reason of our being.

A Friend to You

I would see you as my friend
that I may remember
you are part of me
and come to know myself
by knowing you;
Love myself,
by loving you;
Be myself
the essence of love,
a friend to you.

A Good Day

A good day to know
where
one is going;
Where what seems real,
and what is real, are
the same.

It is no longer necessary
to pinch ourselves to see
if one is awake.
No further looking
behind the curtains,
the veils lie crumpled
at the feet.

It's Only the Mind After All

It is only the mind after all
that holds my brother off
it is only I
thinking in illusion
that binds the world
to false reality
and when I let my thinking free
the world is set free
of its separation.

Muktananda Feast

The day of Swami Muktananda's feast
I thought of you
thinking of your Guru
who strutted through his own kitchen
and sampled and seasoned every pot
everyday

he finished them
in the fire-love
of his Shakti.

Om Shanti

Experience this love which
showers on you
with Baba's thoughts
with Baba's touch
with Baba's heart

You thought it would be
filling to your empty places
and fears
but it overflows as it surrounds you
in magic feelings of God and man
a fleeting glimpse
that we are one
and for an instant
separation is gone
Om Shanti, Shanti.

Muktananda

"Every good thing thou has given unto me;
what oh lord, may I give unto thee?" he asked.
"How may I give the salvation
that has set me free?
How may I give the experiences
by which all may see?"

Nityananda answered,
"Only by seeing thee
as me,
thy heart as mine,
my life as thine."

Within Us

We have within us,
beyond the everyday turmoil,
a place of perpetual peace
illuminated by the light of creation
shining into our life from above.

You Can't Hold On

Life is change
You can't hold on to anything
because there is nothing to hold on to

The universe is a constant creation
the unmanifest converting
into spirit
spirit into energy
energy into matter
in the moment

Nothing that ever was
remains
Everything occurs in this moment

Every cell is renewed
Every light wave becomes a photon
Anti-matter returns to the void

Nothing you hold is real
Nothing you hold is there anymore
just your imagination and memory.

When God Calls

When God calls,
put aside the world
and go where God is

God is within you
go within

Leave the world, and
thoughts of the world, outside

When you are within a vehicle
you are carried along
when you are outside of one
you are trying to keep up

Sit in the seat of your soul
and you will be taken where
the soul is to go.

My Friend Dying

Wisteria intertwined white azaleas
hanging like branches
of pale purple grapes surrounded by butterflies

You were lying so still
with your eyes closed, I thought you were sleeping
but you heard every word said around you

In your frustration
you were living every moment
of your dying.

Litany

We are one being
there is nothing
to fear

ever.

Reality Within The Dream Body

Inside the dream body
our Holy light shines
our strength is a pillar
of God's steel
our soft outer flesh
a rainbow of His Grace

Our eyes are His vision
our lips are the flowers
of His truth
blossoming from
the radiance of our reality.

Breathe the Evening

Breathe the evening air
as amber as the day

The low sun golden
as stalks of grass
on horizon's line

A conscious stream
of breath flows a cool
thread upward
toward the eye
then cascades
down the spine
like a warm spring
waterfall

It leaves the mind
still
the heart full
and feeling God
where it has gone.

Love That Would Last

How do you make love stay?
Leave this world
for this is the transient world
of time and of change
what is held here
will surely pass away
for that which is of this place
is impermanent

If you would
that love would last
take your lover by the hand
and dive into eternity
that your union
might be realized as infinite.

Love III

love is
the only
reality.

Love Is God

Love is God's very being
in love we are one
in love we are God
in God we are love.

Living In a World of My Own Creation

Living in a world of my own creation
the pain of separation
lies only in my mind;
the healing realization of atonement
springs only from my heart.

Time Unreal

Time
is
not.

We Are One

we are one
you and i
there is nothing greater
than our love.

Where Am I

What am I of
but of my creator?

Love has created me
as love

Holiness has made me as
Holy

Light has made me
of light

Love has created me of
its own self.

Being God

If you think you are coming from
or going to
  then you are lost.
If you feel there is anyplace
to come from
or go to
  then you are mistaken.

If you do not think you can exist
in this body without being male or female
you are not experiencing a deep enough state.
For in the depth of your own Self
in deep meditation, honoring and worshiping
your own Self
you discover you no longer feel, nor identify
as male or female
but as being,
as consciousness.

Light, God, Truth, Love, Beauty, Energy, and
Consciousness
are all exactly the same thing,
many names, describing the same oneness

Each person is a portal to the totality of God.
The Kingdom of God dwells within you,
as you.
Every person can know and realize this
it does not matter where someone is from,
or what their sex or creed or religion is,
Every human being can intimately connect
with this,
not simply as a concept
but as an experience.

You have a constant contact with God,
keep touching, concentrating
on that connection
never let go of your contact with God.

Open Your Eyes

Open your eyes and let the world be revealed.
Instead of placing your own judgment
upon it,
gain vision from just a look.
If you withdraw your
own ideas and look with
completely open mind.
the infinite has something to show you,
something beautiful
of infinite value;
hidden under all your thought forms
is you.

Truth

Truth sheds adornments
and runs naked before our eyes
shattering all judgments
and misconceptions

Time cures all lies
no matter how intricate the deception
it is always found out
even the greatest of lies
cannot resist the erosion
of time
for Truth is powerful
and all pervasive
and irresistible
and courses its way through
time
dissolving all falsehoods
and yielding itself to be seen.

Reality –really

There is a certain logic
(quality?)
to a rock
that is so inherent
that it becomes readily apparent
the moment
you see a fake rock.

One Being

We are All One Being

Mahatma Gandhi
knew we were One Being.
He knew it so totally
that he hadn't forgotten it
between the strike of the assassin's bullet
and the touch of the earth where he fell.

Joy of God

The joy of God is pleasuring the heart with love
omnipresent
feeling everywhere love

let it surround you
love from within
let it melt away desires
and fulfill the emptiness
of a space we've held onto too long in this life.

New Year

I sit between the old and new
year
on a day that feels warm
and smells cold;
on a day that joins the two.

I am between the night moon
and coming dawn;
between winter and spring;
neither old nor
any longer young,
I recognize my perspective
and assign lists to be done.

Resolve is my weapon
where there seems no battle at hand
The remaining winter can be gray
and kill you with its grayness
before the tulips ever open
from the earth.

I make lists yet to come
but head each of them
with knowledge of my spirit self.

Forgiveness

God is the love in which
I forgive
and am forgiven.

Identifying with its movement
I am identified with my Guru
who was the incarnating force
of love

And the forgiving
of any who I have condemned
is forgiveness of my mind's portion
which condemns.
It is God's Love, by which I forgive
myself.

What Is God's

All of the love I receive is given
directly to God
I take none of it as for my own

We are just God
loving God

I find all love
is God

And so give to God
what is God's.

The Hard Way

I thought of how all the beings
I have ever loved and helped
could have been helped so much more
by following these instructions
from my Guru

and all those I have traveled to touch
could have been reached
so easily with my spirit body
dematerializing and re-materializing
with the exact instructions
my master has given
that which I do with God's blessing
I would do the hard way
without Master's teachings.

Life

The cycle of life is so perfect
I am constantly given
as I am giving
Like seeds of milkweed in the wind,
the given
is blown back onto me.

Learn From the Child St. Valentine

We learn from the child
who is small and round
and wants to love
who's love is mistreated by the world,
which fails to maintain
their capacity for love

We learn from these small ones
to love unceasingly
and open our Self to the experience
of the world as a plane of love

There is nothing else
but God.
God and love
are all there is.

As long as you think you is
you ain't.
When you realize
you is, then
you Is!

We all Is!

Love as though
we're not we,
but One
Love each other more
than you have ever loved anyone
in your life.

None of it has yet
been enough.
You are much
greater than that

Love as though you are love

We love God with
all our heart and soul
Let us love each other
as though we are One
by this
we are happy and know peace

We experience one wholeness
and there is
nothing less

We remember St. Valentine because
he touched this experience
and invited this love
that you might love, as when you were that small,
round,
child within you.

Papagayo

Suspended in the bay at Papagayo
in a sea of silence
weightless, drifting,
beneath the sun and clouds
not quite sensory deprivation;
there is light,
there is movement,
thread like currents
move over my body
sunlight plays on my eyelids

While drifting in peaceful bliss
I perceive the earth
move slowly on its axis
but the time we measure
by its turning seems
so distant from relevant.

The Heart

My heart is like a dark space
infinite,
alive, with the sparkle of
a million, million suns
twinkling
with encouragement for you.

Embrace everyone
reject no one
we are one being

There is always room
for one more
in the heart.

I am herein
for you

always for you,
existing to offer you
what you will accept

I embrace you
and only you decide
if my embrace be empty or full

It is here for you
If won't you taste it
it will still
be here for you.

Shadow Play

Consciousness is looking out at the world
through the senses,
watching a shadow play caused by the
light of the world on your inner stuff,
your past casting shadows,
neither letting the light of the world in
nor the light of consciousness out
but rather an eclipse
that obstructs both points of perception.

Milky Way and Galaxies

Being serene
with clear eyes open
like windows in a space station
overlooking the Milky Way and galaxies
from a position in space

unfolding the universe
she moves with childlike simplicity
and her hair blows back
with the wind.

God Is One

If we look for truth in world religions
we overlook their discrepancies
and aim for what they all Know as truth,
what they all Know and agree upon.

This my master has taught me.

God is One,
there is only One God and many are the names
but each of the names means that which is The One;
totality,
that which was before creation,
which brought about creation.

To this oneness we ascribe certain attributes
which exist because they are the essence of that totality

Pre-existence:

Before anything was,
That which we called God, existed

Non-duality:

In the beginning there was nothing but God.
When creation was made
there was only God to make it out of
There was not this and that,
not two, only the Creator.
Out of God's own self was creation made.
So, out of God's own self was creation created.

Since in the beginning there was only God
and since God, created the universe, it was out of God,
that substance was wrought into being.
Since everything in creation is derived
from God's being
there is not a thing without God.

Similarly there are certain qualities by which God is
Known universally,
and some lesser being, without these qualities
could not fulfill that which is meant by,
the all-inclusive term, God

These Qualities are:
Omniscience
Omnipotence
Omnipresence

or that
God is all Knowing
All powerful
and everywhere present

Omnipresence

If in the beginning there was no thing
but God
and if all things were made from God
where could there be that God is not present
since each place is made of God's substance, by God?

Omnipotence

Similarly if all that was created
is created from God,
what power in creation can be derived,
but from that creation, which is God?

Omniscience

Finally what would be known
that is not known by God,
for God is the source and substance of all Knowledge?
If it were otherwise, God would not be God.

Then where are we to say God is?
Everywhere – in this book, this tree, this pen,
by what can we see and Know God?

Religion says "God made man in his own image."
Thus, even though God maybe
present in all things, knowledge, and energy,
there is one place where we can see God most easily:
By seeing God in each other

Seeing you, and respecting you as God dwelling within
you,
I see God.
Namaste.

Saints

Like an angel of tears
I see the veil pull back
and something small and
precious open
as love

The movement of this
small force
turns our eyes away
from its awesome presence
and our hearts beat
a little quicker at the feel
of its force

We may be filled
and we may not be Saints yet
but surely we should not
let that stop us from trying
to be holy
toward every person
and take every action
to make them happy,
full of life and peace.

Christmas Poems

A selection of poems written annually over many years.

Light Ye Up Your Candles

Then be ye glad,
good people,
This night of all the year,
And light ye up your candles,
For his star,
it shineth.

From an old English carol

Jesus

Quietly Christmas Eve
after the hymns were sung,
searching closets for gifts,
wrapping presents,
I give each one something
I especially like.
What I can't give up
I take note of

Thinking of you
my heart fills
with love

Loving you
I feel you near
Finding you
I am moved
Seeing you
I drift away from
small thoughts
that play on the edge
of your vast ocean
I become one with all.

Wise Men

Grains of sand beneath
the camel's hoofs
are momentarily displaced
then slide back,
in miniature tan landslides
of a desert evening walk.

Tracks covered by starlight
are soon filled over by wind
as a breeze, ever so lightly,
blows

Olive skin riders,
their capes back, the
pungencies of frankincense
and sandalwood drifts over
their path
Majestic they sit astride
the jostle of beasts, yet
so centered within,
the sky's blue white star
burns in their mind.

Knees pressed against the
fine brocade robe
kneeling in the matted
stable straw
humbly bowed
the struggle is over.
Profound tranquility exists
free of constant demands
of the senses

One with Christ,
duality ceases.
He shines eternally.
Higher-self observing lower-self
is an illusion no longer present
no observation is necessary.

Universal consciousness,
all is one
No longer ego
no longer identification

At the source from which
all creation begins as vibration
world is no longer illusion
but manifestation of the source
one with truth, there remains
only peace and serenity.

Incantation

Among the stubble
of scythed wheat
sat shepherds in
stunned and fearful silence
They heard a hundred thousand voices
sing the Name

Without direction
song seemed to come from every weed
and rock
and tree
from the top
of one another's heads
even from their own sleep
poured praise & glory from
every star,
from the small orange fire,
from their blankets, and sheepskins

Huddled closely they began to see
all around them
beings who flew above the earth to sing

And they closed their eyes
and hid their faces
and still saw all about them
Angels with open mouths proclaim
to them the first blessing was being given.

When they believed
they left their sleep
their fears, their livelihood
behind.

Following the light
they left the darkness
walking
from who they were
to whom they became.

Cornfield Christmas

The bearded shepherd
drifts past
the hustling shoppers
rushing to buy

As the strings of tinsel
drip from the wires
and lamp posts
he wanders from the concrete
into the meadow
now covered
with cold and snow

he looks
at the desolate cornfield and by the flicker
of a dimming star
sees the Christmas.

Within

The joyousness
of Christmas
is experience

The birth of Christ
within
our own eve.

Sun

Warm rains of winter
drizzled over the Holy lands
where father upon father
left foot steps
for sons
now
left only in the legacy
of one generation
to the next

Through the dampness
before dawn
the night clears
over a path a thousand years old
to the back where
the cattle were fed,
near mother and child

Stable walls made of stone,
slender sticks for rafters
hold up the straw roof.

First to wake must have been
the inn keeper's daughters
they dressed and left for water.
Sleepily they made their way to the well and back,
with water jugs on their heads.

The sun
rose colored the ground & walls
the dust was quiet and damp
the inn patrons still asleep
but deep inside the crowded stable
there was no fatigue

those who were weary from their journey
were restored
charged with excitement
energy flowed out from them like
the sun.

Christmas Moonlight

Outside the doorway
a flower is drying
petals turn gold
at the edges.

Trespassing fragments
of transparent clouds
momentarily obscure
patches of moon
then move on.

As if with movement
we nod and look down.
Full moon & stars
shine through my Soul
these eyes are like
windows.

Babe in arms
smiles & smiles
never cries.
On a special Bethlehem morn
everything seems right.

The lyrist sings
    "Christ is born
    in Bethlehem
    and Bethlehem
    is in our heart."

You are blessed this season
you are blessed
the year coming.

God loves you
and Blesses you;
the presence of God
is right within you.

The Christmas Star

The Christmas star,
the crescent moon,
in the quiet
orange of dawn;
an early hour
at father's farm
in a time past,
a Christmas gone.

The earth and sky
dark blue, so still
visionary light
nothing real
except the edge
of a new year
and the promise
in the prayer
for world peace
in which we share.

May Peace Be With You.

After

Brief moments waiting
small seconds spent in the nearest star
are driven away as days resume
their course, only
slightly altered

Following the star
highest graces flowed
like whiffs of frankincense
drifting to coolness
Awakened so briefly,
the consciousness sleeping;
homeward we come
    and away from home we go
    assuming the star will stay with us
    wondering why don't we surrender
    when grace comes,
instead of continuing our own way on.

Headlong Into Christmas

Riding headlong into Christmas
like a passenger in a comfy seat
I feel time pass
as rituals reoccur
in familiar routine
events unfold
I watch them
even as I organize and participate
they still feel other worldly.

Christmas Cookies

Memories of colored lights
like colored sprinkles
over white icing that tastes like vanilla
and the smell of cookies
made from Aunt Elsie's recipe
conjures images of her plump happy demeanor
I can still hear her laugh

My Father, the great jokester
playing games with the presents
hiding marbles in a gift box
to make it rattle
His mother, my grandmother
pinching and shaking each of her gifts
trying to guess what was in them

My sister staying up all night
sewing or knitting some handmade treasure
for Christmas day

My mother up late
trying to jam too much stuffing
into a hollow carcass
and making dish after dish for the feast
so each guest would have their favorite

Then that morning,
the morning awaited,
Mother, up early to start the oven
up early because we were awake
and soon awash in mounds
of shredded wrappings and ribbons

Time for breakfast
and maybe a few more cookies
their bright colored sprinkles
on white icing, streaking
as we dunked them in our milk

Then came the next wave,
grandparents bearing gifts
and more wrappings are shred
as more gifts are opened

Then the next wave of grandparents
and aunts and uncles
and more gifts
and on it went 'til noon

When all had arrived
and we gathered
for the blessing and the eating
and the eating, until
we could eat no more

Then the conversation and coffee
and playtime for the kids
to finally explore all the treasures
we had so hurriedly unwrapped
all the morning long

On this one special day
we didn't have to wash dishes
(though we normally did)
because the women gathered
like a clutch of chickens
around the sink and drainer
and washed and dried and talked and laughed

And the men talked in the living room
and some dozed off for a minute
jerking awake with a start
and looking around to see if anyone noticed

Then when the dishes were dried and done
came the coffee and the pie and deserts
then the cards games and fellowship
until it drew evening.

Someone would ask if we should
put out some slices for sandwiches
and everyone would say
no they were still too full

Eventually the grandparents
and aunts and uncles and cousins
would say it was time to go

We would stand out in the cold
waving as they departed
and the colored lights from the house
would reflect on the snow
in elongated reflections
like the streaks
of colored sprinkles on cookies dipped in milk

And going back into the warm toasty house
We'd say
well maybe, we'll just have a little snack
…some cookies and milk.

Christmas Children

My Daddy loves me
even when he is far
and he is always holding
me in his heart.

When I think of him
or he thinks of me
it fills me with
joy and laughter
for I feel
inside my being
I am his most
beloved daughter.

Well, my Daddy loves me
he is always holding
me
in his heart.

When he thinks of me
or I think of him
it fills me with joy
for I know I am
I am his beloved son,
his favorite boy.

Christmas Poem

The house trimmed for Christmas,
Familiar carols from the stereo,
The warmth of a fire
And of loved ones near,
Their eyes bright with joy.
Images we remember for years.

The most delightful sound I ever hear
Is the sound of my daughter's laughter.
The most beautiful sight to my eyes
Is my son's joy.

It is my hope for your Christmas
That where ever you and your loved ones gather
Your heart will be as full as ours
And your life be as bountifully blessed.

Additional Poetry by Richard Gartee

Mountain Breathing

Collected Poems Volume 2

in paperback and e-book

ISBN: 978-0-9895104-4-8

Canyon Falls

Collected Poems Volume 4

in paperback and e-book

ISBN: 978-0-9895104-7-9

Now available in e-book

Chrysalis

ISBN for e-book edition:

978-0-9895104-0-0

A novel by Richard Gartee

LANCELOT'S GRAIL

in paperback and e-book

ISBN 978-0-9895104-1-7

"Lancelot's spiritual teachings, which constitute the core of this novel, are quite powerful. His eloquence and wisdom resonated over and over again."

—*Erin Wilcox, non-fiction editor, Drunken Boat*

Learn more at:
www.LancelotsGrail.com

About Lancelot's Grail

New age teachings on self-awareness and enlightenment are explored in an Arthurian-age story of two siblings' journey to enlightenment after they discover Sir Lancelot living as a hermit and uncover his knowledge of the Holy Grail.

Sir Lancelot, abandoned by his once-adoring public, has found enlightenment while living as a hermit.

Sir Bedivere, desolate over the knights' abandonment of the Round Table after the fall of Camelot, has come up with a plan.

Alura and Frith, abandoned at an abbey as children, have grown up in social isolation and are desperate for a new life.

Their lives converge when Frith leads Sir Bedivere to Lancelot's hermitage. There, they learn that Lancelot has found the Holy Grail – within himself. Bedivere tries, without success, to persuade Lancelot to come help him rebuild the Knights of The Round Table. After Bedivere departs, Frith begs Lancelot to teach him, hoping to become a knight. Soon Alura joins them, hoping to snare herself a husband.

Lancelot, torn between a desire to be left alone and an obligation to pass his knowledge on, agrees to teach them, but soon realizes that everyone simply wants to use him. Yet, seeing the spark of awareness growing in Alura and Frith, he persists and leads them on a quest to penetrate the barriers in themselves that keep them from attaining the Grail.

Then Alura falls in love with Lancelot and incites an angry mob. Bedivere urges Lancelot to flee, but Lancelot stays, struggling to finish his work with Alura and Frith in the little time he has left.

Under Lancelot's tutelage Alura and Frith come of age, but the ideas presented in Lancelot's Grail invite the reader to reconsider what coming of age really means.

Made in the USA
Charleston, SC
25 October 2013